THE 2023 STAMP YEARBOOK

UNITED STATES POSTAL SERVICE®

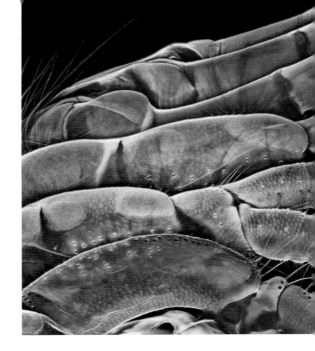

ISBN 978-0-9796569-6-5

Enhance your *2023 Stamp Yearbook* by ordering the mail-use stamps
featured in the second part of this book, which includes 46 stamps plus
mounts (item #992304), and the high-value stamp packet, which includes
3 stamps plus mounts (item #992306).

Order while supplies last at usps.com/shop.

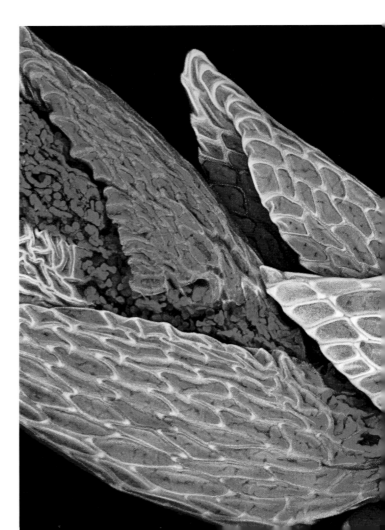

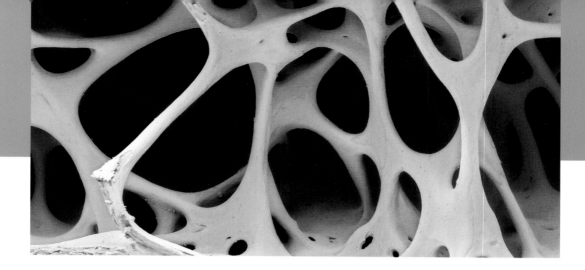

Each stamp reflects a different aspect of American life, inviting us to learn more about history, nature, culture, and the arts. After the Citizens' Stamp Advisory Committee reviews proposals for stamps, a robust creative process begins, as preliminary concepts blossom into an eye-catching array of potential designs. With their expertise and attention to detail, our talented art directors, designers, artists, and researchers transform the suggestions of the public and the committee into a dynamic annual stamp program as multifaceted as the public we serve.

Stamps in 2023 captured the beauty of the world around us in all its myriad forms, from the grandeur of waterfalls and the dignity of endangered species to fascinating images of life at an infinitesimal scale. We remembered leaders whose commitment to justice likewise broadened our national perspective: Native American Chief Standing Bear, civil rights leader and U.S. Congressman John Lewis, and U.S. Supreme Court Justice Ruth Bader Ginsburg.

This year's program brings other aspects of American culture to the forefront as well, highlighting diversity and innovation, history and artistic expression. We celebrated the history and romance of railroad stations, and we recognized the visual ingenuity of skateboard deck art. In this same spirit, we proudly commemorated writers and artists who forever expanded the American mind, including Roy Lichtenstein, an iconic artist of the pop art movement; novelist Ernest J. Gaines, who added a vital African American voice to American literature; prolific children's book author and illustrator Tomie dePaola; and celebrated author, editor, and professor Toni Morrison.

These and the many other subjects featured in the 2023 program have stories to tell, offering new opportunities for discovery, reflection, and celebration. As you read through this collection, I hope you will be inspired by all that we accomplish, both as individuals and as a nation.

Louis DeJoy

Louis DeJoy
Postmaster General and CEO

SECTION ONE

COMM

EMORATIVE
STAMPS

LUNAR NEW YEAR ·
YEAR OF THE RABBIT

LUNAR NEW YEAR
· FOREVER USA ·

ART DIRECTOR & DESIGNER
ANTONIO ALCALÁ

ARTIST
CAMILLE CHEW

PLACE & DATE OF ISSUE
SAN FRANCISCO, CA
JANUARY 12, 2023

"It's an honor to work on a subject that means so much to so many people. I enjoy celebrating parts of our American culture that might not be familiar everywhere in the country."

— *Antonio Alcalá, art director*

In 2023, the fourth of 12 stamps in the latest *Lunar New Year* series was issued in celebration of the Year of the Rabbit.

The rabbit is one of the 12 zodiac animal signs associated with the Chinese lunar calendar. As with other zodiacs, personality traits and other attributes are often associated with people born in the year of a particular animal. Those born during the Year of the Rabbit may be seen as elegant, gracious, and kind.

Lunar New Year is one of the most important holidays for Asian communities around the world and is primarily celebrated by people of Chinese, Korean, Vietnamese, Tibetan, Mongolian, Malaysian, and Filipino heritage. Across these varied cultures, many traditions exist for ringing in a new year of good luck and prosperity.

Art director Antonio Alcalá worked on the *Lunar New Year* stamp series with artist Camille Chew to create imagery that is fresh, fun, and celebratory. Utilizing red, pink, and purple as the predominant colors — said to be lucky colors for individuals born during the Year of the Rabbit — the rabbit mask in the stamp art incorporates elements with symbolic meaning. Several of the patterns evoke the style of Asian textiles, while green flowers represent the arrival of spring. The crescent shape in the center of the rabbit's head references the lunar calendar on which Lunar New Year is based and the celestial themes of the Chinese zodiac.

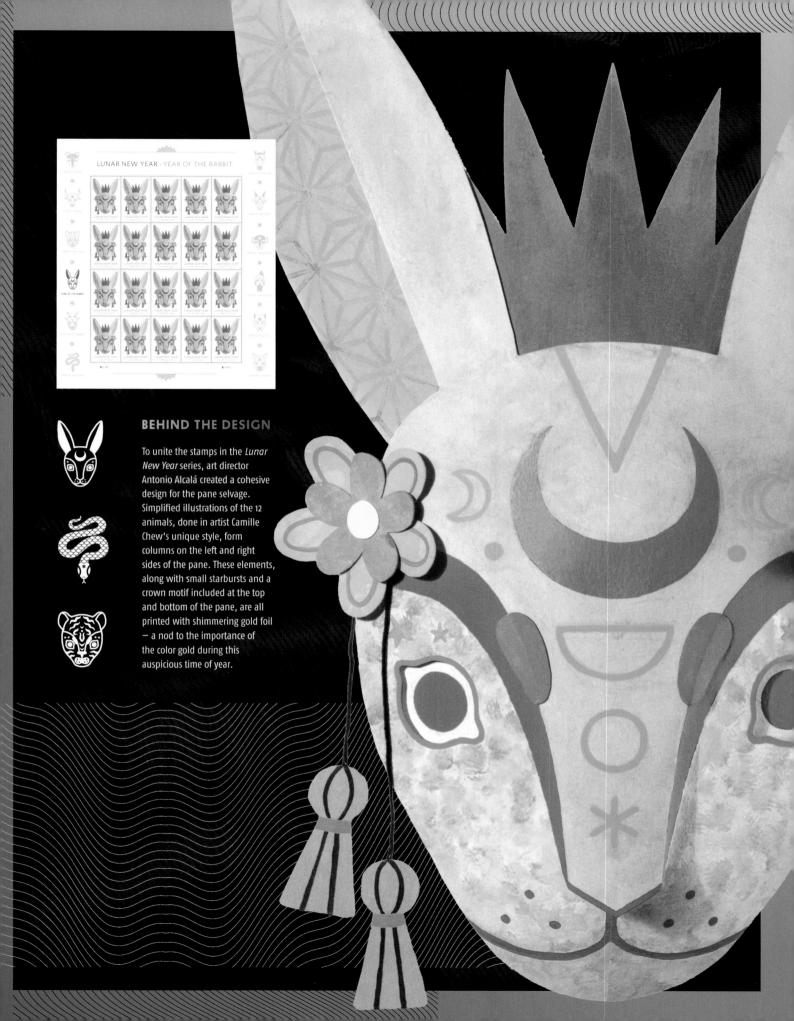

LUNAR NEW YEAR · YEAR OF THE RABBIT

BEHIND THE DESIGN

To unite the stamps in the *Lunar New Year* series, art director Antonio Alcalá created a cohesive design for the pane selvage. Simplified illustrations of the 12 animals, done in artist Camille Chew's unique style, form columns on the left and right sides of the pane. These elements, along with small starbursts and a crown motif included at the top and bottom of the pane, are all printed with shimmering gold foil — a nod to the importance of the color gold during this auspicious time of year.

ARTIST'S CORNER

In 2001, Raoul Benavides had the opportunity to photograph Ernest J. Gaines as part of the author's participation in a reading series hosted by Hennepin County Library in Minnesota.

Benavides, who had a 30-year career as a portrait photographer, was adept at incorporating elements of his subjects' work and persona in his photographs. For Gaines, he chose a location evocative of the rural landscape that serves as the backdrop for much of the author's work. "It was a weird little building, almost in farmland," he recalls. "I thought it was very much Louisiana."

In the short time the two were together they became "intimate chance acquaintances" according to Benavides. "Ernest Gaines was a very pleasant person to be around; I remember us cracking jokes," he says. "He was so great."

BLACK HERITAGE
ERNEST J. GAINES

ART DIRECTOR
GREG BREEDING

DESIGNER
MIKE RYAN

ARTIST
ROBERT PETERSON

PLACE & DATE OF ISSUE
**LAFAYETTE, LA
JANUARY 23, 2023**

"I hope that this stamp inspires other artists and writers of color to go after their dreams. Who would have thought that a young Black kid born in Oscar, LA, in 1933 would end up becoming an award-winning author who would be painted by a Black artist from the small town of Lawton, OK, and it would end up becoming a stamp. It's amazing."

— Robert Peterson, artist

Adding a vital African American voice to American literature, Ernest J. Gaines (1933–2019) brought worldwide attention to generations of men and women who asserted their own dignity in the face of racial oppression and violence.

Best known for such novels as *The Autobiography of Miss Jane Pittman* and *A Lesson Before Dying*, Gaines drew from his childhood as the son of sharecroppers on a Louisiana plantation to explore the many untold stories of rural African Americans. Fascinated by the ways the past inevitably impacts the present, he dramatized the terrible resonance of slavery in Southern society and how it taints the lives of both the descendants of formerly enslaved people and those who had enslaved them.

Early in the creative process for the 46th stamp in the *Black Heritage* series, art director Greg Breeding and designer Mike Ryan decided to work with a portrait artist. They signed on Robert Peterson, who immediately began searching for images of Gaines. A 2001 photograph by Raoul Benavides caught his eye and he set to work capturing the pose, attire, and expression of the author in oil paint on canvas.

"I consider my style of work spontaneous realism, so the process in which the paint is applied is completely random," Peterson says. He brought this unique style and perspective to his portrait of Gaines, while also capturing the writer's spirit.

WOMEN'S SOCCER

ART DIRECTOR & DESIGNER
ANTONIO ALCALÁ

ARTIST
NOAH MACMILLAN

PLACE & DATE OF ISSUE
**ORLANDO, FL
FEBRUARY 16, 2023**

In the United States, women's soccer has gained a firm foothold in sports and popular culture. From youth leagues to the world champion U.S. national team, millions of girls and women across the country participate in the fast-paced, competitive sport.

Despite successes in the years following the passage of Title IX, women's soccer remained relatively unknown until the 1996 Summer Olympics when women's soccer was included as a sport for the first time. The U.S. beat out China for the gold medal. Since then, dozens of elite female athletes have donned the U.S. women's national soccer team jersey and dominated around the world. In 2019, the U.S. made history as the only team to win four FIFA Women's World Cup titles.

Art director Antonio Alcalá worked with artist Noah MacMillan to create a fun, dynamic stamp celebrating women's soccer in the United States. MacMillan started by providing a few sketches with different approaches to the design. "We quickly settled on the one that ended up being the stamp," Alcalá says. "It's a clear image communicating the energy and strength of the players with a nontraditional, unusual perspective."

The stamp artwork depicts a female soccer player in action, walloping a ball with a side volley. Conjuring the aesthetic of mid-century print design, MacMillan used simplified shapes and bold colors to convey the power and speed of the sport. The somewhat grainy rendering lends a timeless quality to the design, evoking not just a single all-star athlete or era but the entire legacy of women's soccer.

"U.S. women's soccer has such an incredible legacy of success; it was humbling to take on as a subject. The U.S. women's national team has made me proud as a fan on and off the field, so I hope some of that comes through."

— Noah MacMillan, artist

ARTIST'S CORNER

Noah MacMillan (1988–2022) had a lifelong passion for soccer. One of his first memories of watching live sporting events as a child was during the 1999 Women's World Cup. In his professional career as a freelance illustrator, he had the opportunity to produce a variety of sports-related work for clients such as Major League Soccer, the Football Association, FIFA, EA Sports, and Adidas. Working on the *Women's Soccer* stamp felt like a culmination of his professional interests as well as his love of the game as both a player and a fan.

PHILATELIC FOCUS

Although Toni Morrison was a literary giant, the stamp recognizing her and her work is not part of the U.S. Postal Service's established *Literary Arts* series. Stamps in the series are now denominated at the three-ounce rate, so a new stamp is issued only when supply runs low. USPS alternates male and female honorees; the most recent stamp in the series celebrated science fiction and fantasy writer Ursula K. Le Guin. All of this meant that a *Literary Arts* stamp for the Nobel laureate would have been a long way off. "We wanted Morrison to stand out on her own as a Forever® stamp," manager of stamp development Shawn Quinn explains, "and be available sooner rather than years from now."

TONI MORRISON

ART DIRECTOR & DESIGNER
ETHEL KESSLER

EXISTING PHOTOGRAPH BY
DEBORAH FEINGOLD

PLACE & DATE OF ISSUE
**PRINCETON, NJ
MARCH 7, 2023**

Eager to write the sorts of novels she had always wanted to find on bookshelves, author, editor, and professor Toni Morrison (1931–2019) explored the diverse voices and multifaceted experiences of African Americans.

Known for such books as *The Bluest Eye*, *Song of Solomon*, and *Beloved*, Morrison was the rare author who achieved both bestseller status and critical success. In 1993, she made history as the first African American woman to win the Nobel Prize in Literature.

Art director Ethel Kessler began the task of honoring Morrison by reading several of her books. "While I knew of her as a writer," Kessler recalls, "I hadn't yet read any of her work firsthand. What an exciting adventure."

After immersing herself in Morrison's words, Kessler pored over the wide array of images of the author, briefly considering working with an artist to have an illustrated portrait created. Her biggest consideration for the stamp was determining the era in which to depict Morrison, a challenge for a public figure whose career spanned decades.

Then Kessler came across a photograph taken by Deborah Feingold of Morrison only a few years after she received the Nobel Prize. "The photo — the color of the background, and her direct gaze — is so compelling that I just couldn't get away from it," she says.

From there she fine-tuned the crop of the image and typography, allowing the portrait of Morrison to shine. "She is powerful inside of the square," Kessler says.

> "Freeing yourself was one thing; claiming ownership of that freed self was another."

— *Toni Morrison,* Beloved *(1987)*

RAILROAD STATIONS

ART DIRECTOR
DERRY NOYES

DESIGNER, ARTIST, & TYPOGRAPHER
DOWN THE STREET DESIGNS

PLACE & DATE OF ISSUE
**CINCINNATI, OH
MARCH 9, 2023**

More than simply places to buy tickets and wait for a train, railroad stations exude history, romance, and the optimism associated with forward motion. Noteworthy stations began brightening the American landscape by the 1870s and, although many fell to the wrecking ball once they had outlived their original purpose, hundreds survived.

Each stamp features an architectural gem that continues to play an important role in its community: the 1874 Tamaqua Station in Tamaqua, Pennsylvania; the 1875 Point of Rocks Station in Point of Rocks, Maryland; the 1901 Main Street Station in Richmond, Virginia; the 1918 Santa Fe Station in San Bernardino, California; and the 1933 Union Terminal in Cincinnati, Ohio.

The United States has hundreds of beautiful old railroad stations, so choosing just five for the stamps posed a dilemma. Art director Derry Noyes knew she wanted architectural diversity, and it was also important to include not just the grandest stations but also some of the smaller ones. In addition, they should all be places people could visit. Once the list was narrowed, Noyes based the final selection on the visual strength of the images, both day and night views, and their overall cohesiveness.

Noyes then enlisted the Los Angeles–based firm Down the Street Designs to illustrate and design the stamps. She had seen their work and knew they could create tiny iconic images for the stations. "I really like the way they distill complex material into simple graphic images," she says.

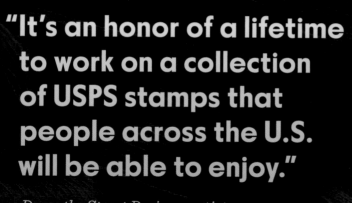

"It's an honor of a lifetime to work on a collection of USPS stamps that people across the U.S. will be able to enjoy."

— Down the Street Designs, artist

BEHIND THE DESIGNS

The Down the Street team created the illustrations for the stamps based on photographs. "We began with grayscale sketches to determine the composition," they explain. "Once those were approved, we produced rough mockups to lock down the shape and color in each illustration." They then painted the compositions using an iPad, trying different colors, and made small finishing touches on the computer.

They designed the pane selvage to resemble a page in an old-fashioned photo album, with the title "Historic Railroad Stations of the United States" and drawings of a train and a one-ride ticket in the header.

"It's an honor of a lifetime to work on a collection of USPS stamps that people across the U.S. will be able to enjoy," the team says.

For each illustration, Down the Street Designs explored a variety of colors to properly capture the building and its environment. "Derry provided us with helpful direction and trusted our creativity," the team says of working with art director Derry Noyes. They created multiple iterations with different palettes and typography, like those shown here for the Point of Rocks Station, before narrowing in on the final designs.

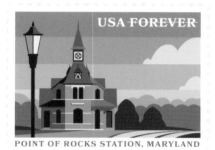

BEHIND THE DESIGNS

Working with four different artists representing vastly different styles and approaches came with its own set of challenges for art director Antonio Alcalá. He wanted each piece of art to stand out on its own and needed to ensure that the set of four stamps worked well together on the pane.

Each of the artists embellished their maple decks with bold designs that convey the excitement of skateboarding while reflecting the diversity and influences of the artists themselves.

"I hope the stamps evoke a sense of joy," Alcalá says. "Skateboarding is a subculture that deserves to be recognized not just for the sport activity, but also for the many creative contributions it makes to our world."

"I am excited to see how the final stamp looks and feels when I hold it, peel it off the paper, and stick it onto an envelope. That sounds really satisfying to me."

— Crystal Worl, artist

ART OF THE SKATEBOARD

ART DIRECTOR & DESIGNER
ANTONIO ALCALÁ

ARTISTS
CRYSTAL WORL
WILLIAM JAMES TAYLOR JUNIOR
DI'ORR GREENWOOD
MASPAZ (FEDERICO FRUM)

PLACE & DATE OF ISSUE
PHOENIX, AZ
MARCH 24, 2023

"Throughout my career I have done many projects, most of them large-scale murals. Never have I worked so hard on a project so small as a stamp that will be printed by the millions!"

— *MasPaz, artist*

Skateboarding skills have advanced leaps and bounds since joyriding youth sparked the craze some six decades ago. A skater's board is highly personal — capable of transforming a mere pedestrian into his or her own vehicle — so its decoration is key.

Bold artwork emblazoned on a skateboard deck is often as eye-catching and individualistic as a skater's most breathtaking moves.

Fiercely independent and often rebellious, the skateboarding subculture crackles with raw creative energy. Dazzling deck art is an integral aspect of skateboarding cool.

Looking to capture the unique visual landscape of skateboard decks, art director Antonio Alcalá worked with artists who have close ties to skateboarding culture to create decks especially for these stamps.

"As you can imagine, each artist had their own working method," he says. "My job was to meet them on their territory. I wanted to make sure they were working in a language that felt authentic and appropriate."

CRYSTAL WORL

Crystal Worl expresses her Indigenous Tlingit/Athabascan heritage with a blue and indigo salmon in her skateboard design, which she rendered in formline, the striking curvilinear style of the northern Northwest Coast. The formline style's origins can be traced back about 2,000 years, having evolved among various Indigenous peoples in the region. Worl, who lives in Juneau, Alaska, advocates modern-day uses of formline by contemporary Indigenous people. Her work explores the relationships and bonds between her people, the land, and the animals.

MasPaz painted a stylized jaguar in black, white, and gold for his skateboard design. His bold strokes respect the traditions of much Indigenous art. The largest cat in the Americas, the jaguar has long symbolized authority and power in the art and lore of Indigenous peoples. As indicated by his Spanish nickname, MasPaz dedicates himself to "more peace" through the content of his artwork and community work, which includes youth programs.

MASPAZ (FEDERICO FRUM)

Arizona native and expert skater Di'Orr Greenwood connects her Navajo and skateboarding cultures in her skateboard design. It includes eagle feathers at the ends, which she points out have great symbolism to both the Navajo and the U.S. Postal Service, its logo a stylized eagle. In the middle of her skateboard design Greenwood painted a colorful burst to evoke the rising or setting sun. The traditional media she used include paint and inlaid crushed turquoise; the dark outlines were rendered with artistic woodburning.

DI'ORR GREENWOOD

A bold graphic abstraction embellishes the deck by self-taught Norfolk, Virginia, artist William James Taylor Junior. His skateboard features a design of red lines and curves against an orange background. He began with many doodled sketches, simplifying his usually dense and frenetic style to read well within the space constraints of the skateboard and the stamp. Taylor has made complex doodles since childhood and is inspired by various artistic styles, including pop art, comic books and cartoons, graffiti, kaleidoscopic images, and psychedelic art.

WILLIAM JAMES TAYLOR JUNIOR

ROY LICHTENSTEIN

Roy Lichtenstein   Roy Lichtenstein   Roy Lichtenstein   Roy Lichtenstein   Roy Lichtenstein

ART DIRECTOR & DESIGNER
DERRY NOYES

EXISTING ART BY
ROY LICHTENSTEIN

PLACE & DATE OF ISSUE
NEW YORK, NY
APRIL 24, 2023

"The importance of art is in the process of doing it, in the learning experience where the artist interacts with whatever is being made."

— Roy Lichtenstein

Roy Lichtenstein (1923–1997), the iconic American artist of the pop art movement, stunned the art world in 1961 with his large paintings starring cartoon characters and a range of consumer products, among other unlikely subjects. Some art connoisseurs found them outrageous, but others saw great meaning in them. Lichtenstein's career quickly took off.

Pop art, which arose in the late 1950s and reached its height in the 1960s, looked to popular culture for its aesthetic. It often was seen as poking fun at consumerism.

With their trademark heavy black outlining, intense colors, dot pattern simulating the benday dot printing process used in the 1960s for comic books and magazines, and machine-made quality, Lichtenstein's paintings are instantly recognizable.

Lichtenstein went on to explore many genres, including Cubism, Purism, and Futurism. The many honors he received over the course of his career include induction into the American Academy of Arts and Letters in 1979 and the National Medal of Arts in 1995.

Commemorating the artist and his work brought newfound appreciation for art director Derry Noyes, who thoroughly researched Lichtenstein's history and oeuvre. "Here is a man with a vision and a voice," she explains. "He had a sense of irony — playful, intentional. He clearly loved going to the studio to work/play every day."

After poring over the artist's body of work, Noyes chose five pieces of Lichtenstein's art to showcase on the stamps — two still lifes, a portrait, a sculpture, and an abstract painting. While she acknowledges the difficulty of distilling an entire career into five images, Noyes believes "overall, one gets the energy, the zest, and the expanse of Lichtenstein's work through these pieces of art."

Still Life with Goldfish (1972) is an acrylic, oil, and graphite pencil on canvas painting that is owned by a private collector.

Standing Explosion (Red) (1965) is a porcelain enamel on steel work that is part of the collection of the Crystal Bridges Museum of American Art, in Bentonville, Arkansas.

Modern Painting I (1966) is an acrylic, oil, and graphite pencil on canvas painting that is part of the collection of the Frederick R. Weisman Art Foundation, in Los Angeles, California.

Still Life with Crystal Bowl (1972) is an acrylic, oil, and graphite pencil on canvas painting that is part of the collection of the Whitney Museum of American Art, in New York City.

BEHIND THE DESIGNS

To fully honor the breadth and depth of Roy Lichtenstein and his work, art director Derry Noyes tried to incorporate a variety of media and styles while also creating visual unity for the stamp pane. "His exploration and experimentation in sculpture as well as painting were huge, let alone the volume of his work," Noyes says. "It was a juggling act."

She narrowed her selection to Lichtenstein pieces that would work well in a vertical format. Upon finding a photograph by Bob Adelman of Lichtenstein standing in front of one of his dot-pattern paintings, Noyes felt the pane coming together. "It has the key elements in it — the primary colors, the benday dots, the strong graphic strokes, and the energy," she explains. "And it's a particularly appealing portrait of the man who made this art."

Portrait of a Woman (1979) is an acrylic, oil, and graphite pencil on canvas painting that is owned by a private collector.

"These stamps are a glimpse into an artist that I hope will encourage more in-depth exploration. He was quite a force."

— *Derry Noyes, art director*

PHILATELIC FOCUS

Tomie dePaola joins a venerable group of
children's book authors and illustrators
and their creations commemorated on
stamps. USPS honored the extraordinarily
versatile Shel Silverstein in 2022 with a stamp
featuring an image from the cover of his
picture book *The Giving Tree*. Four stamps
in 2017 celebrated Ezra Jack Keats's most
beloved story *The Snowy Day*. A 2006 pane
featured eight cherished animal characters
from children's literature — The Very Hungry
Caterpillar (Eric Carle), Maisy (Lucy Cousins),
Curious George (Margret and H.A. Rey), Olivia
(Ian Falconer), Wild Thing (Maurice Sendak),
Wilbur (illustrator Garth Williams), Frederick
(Leo Lionni), and Fox in Socks (Dr. Seuss).

TOMIE DEPAOLA

ART DIRECTOR & DESIGNER
DERRY NOYES

EXISTING ART BY
TOMIE DEPAOLA

PLACE & DATE OF ISSUE
MANCHESTER, NH
MAY 5, 2023

"So often we have 'head' stamps when honoring people. We hire artists to render their portraits or use photography. In this case we could use the actual work of the person we are honoring. The art, stories, and characters Tomie created will live on forever."

— *Derry Noyes, art director*

Prolific children's book author and illustrator Tomie dePaola (1934–2020) produced an extraordinarily varied body of work that encompasses folktales and legends, informational books, religious and holiday stories, and touching autobiographical tales.

DePaola is probably best known for the Strega Nona picture book series. Set in southern Italy, the gently humorous stories focus on Strega Nona, "Grandma Witch," who uses magic to help with matters of the heart and to cure her neighbors' ills.

Having spent countless hours reading these books to her children when they were young, art director Derry Noyes felt a nostalgic connection to the character and her creator while working on this project. She quickly focused on a detail from the cover of *Strega Nona*, the first book in the series. Published in 1975, the book received a Caldecott Honor as one of the most distinguished picture books published that year.

"This image captures the very essence of all the Strega Nona books," Noyes explains. "It also works well at stamp size and depicts dePaola's most famous character at her house, with her pasta pot, surrounded by animals." From there, Noyes selected a font for dePaola's name compatible with the illustration. In the top of the pane selvage, she placed dePaola's signature — simply "Tomie" with a heart — as a sign-off from the author and illustrator himself.

CHIEF STANDING BEAR

ART DIRECTOR, DESIGNER, & TYPOGRAPHER
DERRY NOYES

ARTIST
THOMAS BLACKSHEAR II

PLACE & DATE OF ISSUE
LINCOLN, NE
MAY 12, 2023

A leader of the Ponca tribe, Chief Standing Bear (ca 1829–1908) won a landmark court ruling that determined a Native American was a person under the law with an inherent right to life, liberty, and the pursuit of happiness.

In 1877, the U.S. Army had forcibly relocated some 700 Ponca to Indian Territory (Oklahoma) after the federal government had given away the tribe's homeland in the Niobrara River Valley in what is now northeastern Nebraska.

Chief Standing Bear and some of his followers were arrested after attempting to return to their homeland. In a landmark civil rights case, *Standing Bear* v. *Crook*, lawyers filed for a writ of habeas corpus to test the legality of his detention, an unprecedented filing on behalf of a Native American. After winning the case, Standing Bear returned to his old Nebraska reservation.

Artist Thomas Blackshear II based his portrait on a black-and-white photograph taken of Standing Bear in 1877 while he was in Washington, D.C., as part of a delegation of Ponca chiefs. Blackshear drew upon a 19th-century account of Standing Bear's appearance at his trial when he added color to the chief's face and attire.

"I feel as if Thomas's portrait conveys the inner soul of this extraordinary man," art director Derry Noyes says. "I thought the portrait was so powerful and his story so compelling, I decided to blow it up large and place it in the selvage as well to draw the viewer in. It's hard not to be moved by it."

> "I thought the portrait was so powerful and his story so compelling, I decided to blow it up large and place it in the selvage as well to draw the viewer in. It's hard not to be moved by it."

— *Derry Noyes, art director*

PHILATELIC FOCUS

Artist Thomas Blackshear II is known for his dramatic lighting and sensitivity to mood. Particularly adept at portraiture, he has created numerous stamp designs for the U.S. Postal Service, including five stamps in the *Black Heritage* series, most recently the 2017 stamp honoring Dorothy Height. In addition, his artwork has been featured on more than a dozen stamps commemorating classic films (1990), James Baldwin (2004), Mother Teresa (2010), and Rosa Parks (2013). Twenty-eight of his depictions of famous Black Americans are featured in the 1992 *Black Heritage* series commemorative book entitled *I Have a Dream*.

"If we think that we can throw half of these animals away to extinction and that we'll be just fine, that's not accurate. It's just not going to work out that way."

— *Joel Sartore, conservation photographer*

ENDANGERED SPECIES

ART DIRECTOR & DESIGNER
DERRY NOYES

EXISTING PHOTOGRAPHS BY
JOEL SARTORE

PLACE & DATE OF ISSUE
WALL, SD
MAY 19, 2023

America's natural bounty includes an astounding variety of unique wildlife. Under the Endangered Species Act (ESA), which marks its 50th anniversary in 2023, more than 1,600 imperiled plant and animal species are safeguarded to increase their chances of survival.

The ESA's protections are effective. Scientists estimate that hundreds of species have been rescued from the brink of extinction. Many species including our national symbol, the bald eagle, and the American alligator have rebounded with such success that they no longer require ESA protections. The stamps feature a sampling of endangered species found within the 50 states and American territories and possessions, and also include two North American species living near U.S. borders.

Showcasing representative mammal, bird, fish, amphibian, reptile, and crustacean species across such a wide geographic range was no easy task for art director Derry Noyes. "Fortunately, I had a lot to work with," she says. Noyes looked through thousands of photographer Joel Sartore's striking images. "The photographs are incredibly powerful. It was a joy to have so many to work with that would make beautiful stamps."

In addition to species and geographic diversity, it was also important to include a few extreme close-up images of animals, both from a subject and design perspective. "Seeing their expressions draws on our emotions," Noyes explains. "And visually the pane is more interesting with different angles and points of view."

"This is a subject that is not going away. Beautiful stamps are a simple and effective method to keep the subject of endangered species alive."

— *Derry Noyes, art director*

ARTIST'S CORNER

The colorful and charismatic creatures featured on the stamps are among more than 16,000 represented in photographer Joel Sartore's "Photo Ark" project, his enduring mission to document as many animal species as possible, from all over the world. Sartore's studio-style portraits give vivid immediacy to the uniqueness of each individual pictured and to the species it represents.

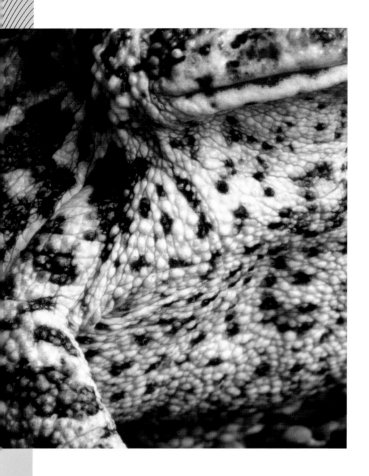

The five rows of stamps each feature four different species:

FIRST ROW: Laysan teal *(Anas laysanensis)*, black-footed ferret *(Mustela nigripes)*, Roanoke logperch *(Percina rex)*, and thick-billed parrot *(Rhynchopsitta pachyrhyncha)*

SECOND ROW: candy darter *(Etheostoma osburni)*, Florida panther *(Puma concolor couguar)*, masked bobwhite quail *(Colinus virginianus ridgwayi)*, and Key Largo cotton mouse *(Peromyscus gossypinus allapaticola)*

THIRD ROW: Lower Keys marsh rabbit *(Sylvilagus palustris hefneri)*, Wyoming toad *(Anaxyrus baxteri)*, Vancouver Island marmot *(Marmota vancouverensis)*, and golden-cheeked warbler *(Setophaga chrysoparia)*

FOURTH ROW: Guam Micronesian kingfisher *(Halcyon cinnamomina cinnamomina)*, San Francisco garter snake *(Thamnophis sirtalis tetrataenia)*, Mexican gray wolf *(Canis lupus baileyi)*, and Attwater's prairie chicken *(Tympanuchus cupido attwateri)*

FIFTH ROW: Nashville crayfish *(Faxonius shoupi)*, piping plover *(Charadrius melodus)*, desert bighorn sheep *(Ovis canadensis nelsoni)*, and Mississippi sandhill crane *(Grus canadensis pulla)*

Endangered Species

Laysan teal 	*Black-footed ferret* 	*Roanoke logperch* 	*Thick-billed parrot* 
Candy darter 	*Florida panther* 	*Masked bobwhite quail* 	*Key Largo cotton mouse* 
Lower Keys marsh rabbit 	*Wyoming toad* 	*Vancouver Island marmot* 	*Golden-cheeked warbler* 
Guam Micronesian kingfisher 	*San Francisco garter snake* 	*Mexican gray wolf* 	*Attwater's prairie chicken* 
Nashville crayfish 	*Piping plover* 	*Desert bighorn sheep* 	*Mississippi sandhill crane* 

B11111   B11111

WATERFALLS

Harrison Wright Falls, Pennsylvania

ART DIRECTOR & DESIGNER
GREG BREEDING

EXISTING PHOTOGRAPHS BY
VARIOUS PHOTOGRAPHERS

PLACE & DATE OF ISSUE
YELLOWSTONE NATIONAL PARK, WY
JUNE 13, 2023

Among nature's most beautiful wonders, waterfalls come in all shapes and sizes, from serene cascades to mighty cataracts. A perennial favorite of photographers, amateur and professional, the visual beauty of waterfalls and their natural surroundings is not their only appeal. The sound of the falling water — whether a melodic trickle or a thunderous roar — also draws visitors.

The 12 waterfalls featured on these stamps represent many different types, and each is unique. What they all have in common is the way they kindle positive emotions, such as the serenity instilled by a gentle cascade or the awe inspired by an immense cataract.

The design direction began to take shape after art director Greg Breeding pored over hundreds of images provided by image research, rights, and permissions expert Michael Owens. "I quickly learned there are way more waterfalls in the United States than I realized," Breeding recalls. "And it seemed obvious to pursue photography since waterfalls make for such arresting imagery."

Breeding sought geographic and visual diversity in the photos he selected, wanting to represent the country's varied regions and climates. He then arranged the images on the pane with an emphasis on highlighting the unique qualities of each waterfall, cropping some to show only a detail while others include the entire waterfall.

> "I quickly learned there are way more waterfalls in the United States than I realized. And it seemed obvious to pursue photography since waterfalls make for such arresting imagery."

— Greg Breeding, art director

"Yosemite and its familiar landmarks evoke images made by the great names in photographic history. I found my own unmediated inspiration in the landscape with the rushing waters of Nevada Fall and towering cliffs of Liberty Cap, and in my feelings of awe and belonging."

— QT Luong, photographer

BEHIND THE DESIGNS

Art director Greg Breeding arranged his selection of waterfalls in three rows of four stamps on the pane.

FIRST ROW: Deer Creek Falls, Grand Canyon National Park, Arizona; Nevada Fall, Yosemite National Park, California; Harrison Wright Falls, Ricketts Glen State Park, Pennsylvania; and Lower Falls of the Yellowstone River, Yellowstone National Park, Wyoming

SECOND ROW: Waimoku Falls, Haleakalā National Park, Hawai'i; Stewart Falls, Mount Timpanogos Wilderness, Utah; Niagara Falls, Niagara Falls State Park, New York; and Dark Hollow Falls, Shenandoah National Park, Virginia

THIRD ROW: Grotto Falls, Great Smoky Mountains National Park, Tennessee; Sunbeam Falls, Mount Rainier National Park, Washington; LaSalle Canyon Waterfall, Starved Rock State Park, Illinois; and Upper Falls, Blue Ridge Parkway, North Carolina

BEHIND THE DESIGN

In addition to the powerful photograph of John Lewis taken later in his life that she chose for the stamp, art director Derry Noyes also wanted to depict Lewis at a younger age to make clear his lifelong commitment to fighting racial oppression. "It's not easy to get that across with just one stamp," Noyes explains.

To satisfy this design challenge, she decided to use an older photograph of Lewis on the pane selvage. The black-and-white image she selected was taken by Steve Schapiro in 1963 — 50 years prior to the Marco Grob photograph on the stamp — outside a workshop about nonviolent protest in Clarksdale, Mississippi. (Lewis later told Schapiro that the black-and-white portrait was one of his favorite photos of himself.)

"He was working for this cause for most of his life," Noyes says. "It was an honor to commemorate a person I admire this much."

JOHN LEWIS

ART DIRECTOR & DESIGNER
DERRY NOYES

EXISTING PHOTOGRAPH BY
MARCO GROB

PLACE & DATE OF ISSUE
ATLANTA, GA
JULY 21, 2023

A key figure in some of the most pivotal moments of the civil rights movement, John Lewis (1940–2020) was the face of the Nashville Student Movement, chairman of the Student Nonviolent Coordinating Committee, an original Freedom Rider, and one of the keynote speakers at the historic 1963 March on Washington. Even in the face of hatred and violence, Lewis remained resolute in his commitment to what he liked to call "good trouble."

Devoted to equality and justice for all Americans, Lewis spent more than 30 years in the U.S. Congress steadfastly defending and building on key civil rights gains of the 1960s. He also worked for more than a decade to establish the National Museum of African American History and Culture on the National Mall in Washington, D.C.

When art director Derry Noyes began working on honoring Lewis, she initially considered signing on an artist to create an illustrated portrait. Then she found a photograph of the civil rights icon that changed her mind — taken by Marco Grob for the August 26, 2013, issue of *TIME* magazine. "His direct gaze and the dramatic lighting are so powerful," Noyes says. "The image exudes everything about the man."

She chose a bold typeface for displaying Lewis's name that complements the photo without detracting from it. "His resolute, inner strength comes through loud and clear," Noyes says.

"The vote is precious — it is almost sacred. It is the most powerful nonviolent tool we have in a democratic society, and we have to use it."

— *Congressman John Lewis*

LIFE MAGNIFIED

ART DIRECTOR & DESIGNER
DERRY NOYES

EXISTING PHOTOGRAPHS BY
VARIOUS PHOTOGRAPHERS

PLACE & DATE OF ISSUE
CLEVELAND, OH
AUGUST 10, 2023

With 20 otherworldly images, these stamps explore life on Earth, as few have ever seen it. The pane features images taken using microscopes and highly specialized photographic techniques to capture details of life undetectable by the human eye.

Scientists have long held deep fascination with making the invisible elements of our world visible. The images that result from microscope-based research show, in exquisitely fine detail, the phenomena of life. By incorporating aesthetic appeal into the ways they present their research, scientists have created images equally suited for a gallery wall as for a scientific journal. Their work reveals the grandeur of life at an infinitesimal scale.

For art director Derry Noyes, working on these stamps brought immense fascination. "The extraordinary beauty of these photos made it so fun as well as educational," she recalls. After looking through dozens of world-class photomicrography images in her research, she decided to focus specifically on images that show elements of life.

From there she made her selections with balance in mind, incorporating a variety of subjects, looking for visual diversity, and always considering which images would be most legible at stamp size. "The surprise factor is what makes these stamps so unusual," Noyes says. "I hope they spark curiosity and the bit of wow that hit me while I was working on this project."

> "The surprise factor is what makes these stamps so unusual. I hope they spark curiosity and the bit of wow that hit me while I was working on this project."
>
> — *Derry Noyes, art director*

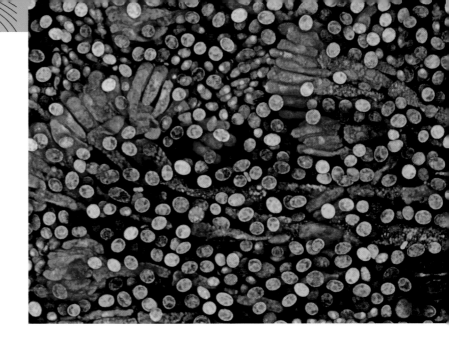

SCIENTIST'S CORNER

While stunning on their own as works of art, images that result from microscope-based research also hold scientific significance. Daniel Castranova, an aquatic research specialist working with the National Institutes of Health, made an image of a juvenile zebrafish using confocal microscopy, a process that scans a specimen to create several optical sections of the subject. These sections are then stacked to provide an extended depth of field giving the impression of a three-dimensional reconstruction of the subject.

Castranova's zebrafish image reveals the presence of lymphatic vessels within the fish's skull, previously never observed in the skulls of non-mammals. This groundbreaking discovery may help scientists form a better understanding of human diseases.

LIFE MAGNIFIED

Red Blood Cells — FOREVER / USA

Macaw Parrot Feather — FOREVER / USA

Human Hair — FOREVER / USA

Moss Leaves — FOREVER / USA

Arranged Diatoms — FOREVER / USA

Freshwater Protozoans — FOREVER / USA

Acorn Barnacle — FOREVER / USA

Moth Antenna — FOREVER / USA

Diving Beetle Front Foot — FOREVER / USA

Mouse Brain Neurons — FOREVER / USA

Starling Bone Tissue — FOREVER / USA

Moth Wing Scales — FOREVER / USA

Zebrafish — FOREVER / USA

Mushroom Gills — FOREVER / USA

Freshwater Snail Tongue — FOREVER / USA

Blue Button Organism — FOREVER / USA

Mold Spores — FOREVER / USA

Barnacle Legs — FOREVER / USA

Flame Lily Pollen — FOREVER / USA

Oak Leaf Surface — FOREVER / USA

B1111   B1111

The five rows of four stamps each feature four different images:

FIRST ROW: red blood cells, the feather of a macaw parrot, a knotted strand of human hair, and moss leaves

SECOND ROW: diatom shells (photosynthesizing algae), freshwater protozoans, an acorn barnacle, and a moth's antenna

THIRD ROW: the front foot of a diving beetle, neurons from a mouse's brain, bone tissue from a starling, and scales on the wing of a Madagascan sunset moth

FOURTH ROW: a juvenile zebrafish, mushroom gills, the tongue of a freshwater snail, and a blue button (an organism similar to a jellyfish)

FIFTH ROW: mold spores, the legs (known as cirri) of a barnacle, flame lily pollen, and the surface of a southern live oak leaf

BEHIND THE DESIGNS

Encouraged by the success of the *From Me to You* stamp in 2015 and *Message Monsters* in 2021, both of which included die-cut images on the pane selvage for decorating envelopes, art director Greg Breeding designed the stamp pane with words of encouragement and thoughtful affirmations surrounding the stamps. Displayed in the same muted tones used throughout the stamp designs, each greeting is die-cut and self-adhesive to further enhance messages and add a special touch to envelopes.

"There's an appetite for playful ways to enliven communication," Breeding says. "I hope these stamps inspire people to send positive messages to friends and family."

THINKING OF YOU

ART DIRECTOR & DESIGNER
GREG BREEDING

ILLUSTRATOR
ELLEN SURREY

PLACE & DATE OF ISSUE
CLEVELAND, OH
AUGUST 11, 2023

"There's a joy to the stamps. They make you smile. When I was a kid, I loved getting mail. There was something very special about getting a card or letter that was addressed to you, and that's the feeling we were trying to capture."

— *Ellen Surrey, illustrator*

Whether sending a note of celebration, gratitude, or just to say hi, letting those we care about know that we're thinking of them affirms our love and affection. In good times and bad, checking in on friends and family provides an important connection. A feel-good, handwritten message of any length can boost spirits and bring relationships closer, despite miles of distance.

Wanting to capture the delight of receiving a card in the mail meant just for you, art director Greg Breeding worked with illustrator Ellen Surrey to create a bevy of bright, uplifting icons appropriate for any occasion. "Ellen's work can be quite sophisticated but is almost always playful and friendly," Breeding says, just the balance he wanted to strike with these stamps.

The two collaborated on the icons that would work best. "We wanted the stamps to be useful all year long," Surrey explains, "not just for Valentine's Day or an anniversary." Working digitally to create each illustration, she also chose a cohesive color palette to bring the disparate icons together. Breeding then arranged them in the stamp format, creating fun and somewhat unexpected combinations of whimsical images.

OSIRIS-REx

ART DIRECTOR & DESIGNER
ANTONIO ALCALÁ

ARTIST
ALAN DINGMAN

PLACE & DATE OF ISSUE
**SALT LAKE CITY, UT
SEPTEMBER 22, 2023**

NASA's seven-year OSIRIS-REx mission to study and map the asteroid Bennu ended September 24, 2023, with the return to Earth of a sample of the asteroid's surface. This is the first pristine sample of an asteroid collected by the United States, and it will help scientists learn how our solar system formed.

OSIRIS-REx left Earth aboard a rocket launched from Cape Canaveral, Florida, on September 8, 2016. After it arrived in the asteroid's orbit, in December 2018, it began photographing and mapping Bennu's surface to determine the best site from which to collect the sample. In October 2020 the spacecraft descended toward Bennu and, without landing, extended a robotic arm to capture a few ounces of material.

On May 10, 2021, OSIRIS-REx began its flight back toward Earth. Its capsule of asteroid dust and rocks parachuted down to the Utah desert more than two years later.

Art director Antonio Alcalá sketched out a few ideas for the stamp, based on information from NASA, before settling on a design direction. "Since USPS was planning to issue the stamp around the date of the sample return, that was the moment I chose to commemorate on the stamp itself," Alcalá says. NASA and its partners had produced a series of images and animations to illustrate the mission. Alcalá provided these to artist Alan Dingman, who then created the artwork for the stamp and the pane.

"Since USPS was planning to issue the date of the sample return, that was the moment I chose to commemorate on the stamp itself."

— *Antonio Alcalá, art director*

1 EARTH'S GRAVITY PUSHES
OSIRIS-REx TO BENNU

2 OSIRIS-REx
MAPS ASTEROID

3 OSIRIS-REx ORBITS,
THEN DESCENDS TO BENNU

4 OSIRIS-REx
COLLECTS SAMPLE

BEHIND THE DESIGN

Conversations with NASA staff early in the design process revealed that the OSIRIS-REx mission had five important milestones: using Earth's gravity to boost the spacecraft on its path toward Bennu; mapping the asteroid; descending toward Bennu; collecting a sample of its surface; and returning the sample capsule to Earth.

Having decided to depict the return to Earth on the stamp, art director Antonio Alcalá used the pane selvage to illustrate the entire mission. In addition to images of the four other milestones and of Bennu, the selvage includes a close-up of Bennu's surface with outer space above, deep blue and dappled with celestial bodies.

BEHIND THE DESIGN

Like her fellow justice Sandra Day O'Connor, the first woman on the Supreme Court of the United States, Ruth Bader Ginsburg decorated her judicial robe with a lace collar. Her ornamental collars, especially the one she chose to wear when she dissented, would define the justice's image in the mind of the public for years to come.

Ginsburg's favorite collar, purchased in South Africa in 2006, featured a repeating diamond pattern and beadwork. She wore it to President Barack Obama's State of the Union address in 2012, in her official Supreme Court portrait, and in a photograph that appeared on the cover of *TIME.* Artist Michael J. Deas used a facsimile of this collar as reference to correctly capture its drapery in his painting of the justice.

RUTH BADER GINSBURG

ART DIRECTOR & DESIGNER
ETHEL KESSLER

ARTIST
MICHAEL J. DEAS

PLACE & DATE OF ISSUE
WASHINGTON, D.C.
OCTOBER 2, 2023

Ruth Bader Ginsburg (1933–2020) served as the 107th Supreme Court Justice of the United States. After beginning her career as an activist lawyer fighting gender discrimination, Ginsburg became a respected jurist whose important opinions advancing gender equality and strong dissents on socially controversial rulings expressed her passionate advocacy of equal justice under law and made her an icon of American culture.

Ginsburg's multifaceted legacy includes the legal and social changes she helped to bring about during her long career; the example she set of tenacity and perseverance in the service of meaningful work; the inspiring passion that she brought to her dissents in defense of principles she held dear; and the countless people who view her as a role model for their own lives.

Commemorating Ginsburg held deep meaning for art director Ethel Kessler. "It was such an honor working on this project," she says, being tasked with depicting "someone who is so revered in the women's movement, legal circles, and as a human being." Kessler signed on award-winning illustrator and master realist artist Michael J. Deas to create the portrait. Deas provided several detailed pencil sketches before making the final oil painting based on a photograph by Philip Bermingham.

"There are several very fine photographic portraits of Ginsburg," Kessler notes, "but to my eye, the painted portrait is everlasting and a look into the soul."

> **"It was such an honor working on this project. Ruth Bader Ginsburg is someone who is so revered in the women's movement, legal circles, and as a human being."**
>
> *— Ethel Kessler, art director*

MAIL-USE STAMPS

LOVE

ART DIRECTOR, DESIGNER, & TYPOGRAPHER
ETHEL KESSLER

ARTIST
CHRIS BUZELLI

PLACE & DATE OF ISSUE
AUSTIN, TX
JANUARY 19, 2023

Evoking feelings of affection and playfulness, the latest *Love* stamps coincide with the 50th anniversary of the ever popular series. This year's stamps feature illustrations of a kitten and a puppy by artist Chris Buzelli.

"When I got the initial call for the project," recalls Buzelli, "I sat down and quickly sketched out close to 100 thumbnail ideas." After narrowing the possibilities down to about 20, Buzelli worked with art director Ethel Kessler to finalize the design. Together they settled on one of the artist's earliest concepts, an image of a puppy. Kessler also asked for a companion design featuring a kitten.

Describing his style as a mix of realism and fantasy, Buzelli painted each image using oil on wood board, giving the art texture and warmth. He then scanned each painting so that he could edit them digitally and add finishing touches.

"I'm not sure how to explain it," says Buzelli when asked about the bond that humans enjoy with cats and dogs, "but there is something so innate and internal that happens when you see a puppy or kitten. It's an immediate feeling of cuteness, warmth, kindness, and affection. I guess it's called love."

"There is something so innate and internal that happens when you see a puppy or kitten. It's an immediate feeling of cuteness, warmth, kindness, and affection. I guess it's called love."

— *Chris Buzelli, artist*

TULIP BLOSSOMS

ART DIRECTOR & DESIGNER
GREG BREEDING

EXISTING PHOTOGRAPHS BY
DENISE IPPOLITO

PLACE & DATE OF ISSUE
WOODBURN, OR
APRIL 5, 2023

Each fall, millions of gardeners bury bulbs in the earth, eagerly anticipating the rewards that springtime will bring. Months later, thick green leaves poke through the soil, soon revealing their payload: tulip blossoms in spectacular variety, from prim to ostentatious.

Dutch immigrants brought tulip bulbs to America, perhaps as early as the 1600s. Since then, the flower has become a dazzling part of the landscape, with seemingly endless varieties grown in gardens across most of the country.

"What immediately drew me to Denise's images was the sense of scale — how close she was able to get to the tulips," explains art director Greg Breeding. "There is a subtleness in how she has chosen to focus on the petals that I find very beautiful."

Because the tulips were photographed at such close range, the design work proved somewhat challenging. "They are beautiful even in abstraction," says Breeding, "but I still wanted them to be recognized as actual flowers." To do that, he cropped the images to reveal little details to better identify them as tulips. Each stamp features one flower, filling almost the entire frame with just the top of the stem showing.

"I think these stamps have a kind of quiet beauty," Breeding reflects. "They are understated but also colorful."

U.S. FLAG

ART DIRECTOR & DESIGNER
ANTONIO ALCALÁ

EXISTING ART BY
HONG LI

PLACE & DATE OF ISSUE
FREEDOM, ME
APRIL 10, 2023

An important symbol of our nation, the U.S. flag serves as a visual reminder of the array of liberties that Americans enjoy. "Freedom is a concept that continues to resonate," reflects art director Antonio Alcalá. "It's one of our most cherished ideals." The widespread appeal of the flag is suggested by the versatility of this stamp, which will be sold in booklets of 20, panes of 20, and coils of 100, 3,000, and 10,000.

PATRIOTIC BLOCK

ART DIRECTOR
ANTONIO ALCALÁ

DESIGNER
CAROL BEEHLER

PLACE & DATE OF ISSUE
LIBERTY, NY
MARCH 1, 2023

The star-spangled banner has appeared regularly on postage stamps over the years. "It makes sense to feature the U.S. flag," explains art director Antonio Alcalá, "but presenting it in new, creative ways while also honoring its legacy can be challenging." It's a challenge he both enjoys and respects. For this nondenominated, nonprofit-price stamp, Alcalá worked with designer Carol Beehler, who arranged the components of the flag — the stars and stripes — in a four-quadrant block.

BRIDGES

ART DIRECTOR & DESIGNER
ETHEL KESSLER

EXISTING PHOTOGRAPHS BY
VARIOUS PHOTOGRAPHERS

PLACE & DATE OF ISSUE
PORTLAND, CT
AUGUST 24, 2023

Among the oldest structures created by humans, bridges have evolved from utilitarian designs to engineering marvels. Whether simply improving transit or vibrantly lighting the night with color-changing displays, their construction can help reinvigorate local economies and stimulate regional pride. Today, with more than 600,000 bridges in the United States, they remain as integral to American life as ever.

These stamps feature photographs of four bridges completed between 1938 and 2022, including a multi-span steel through arch bridge, an s-curved cable-stayed pedestrian bridge, a steel truss structure topped by a public sculpture, and a "basket-handle" twin-arch bridge. Ranging from historic to modern, pedestrian to car-carrying, all four bridges are important landmarks in their communities.

PIÑATAS!

ART DIRECTOR
ANTONIO ALCALÁ

DESIGNER & ARTIST
VÍCTOR MELÉNDEZ

PLACE & DATE OF ISSUE
**ROSWELL, NM
SEPTEMBER 8, 2023**

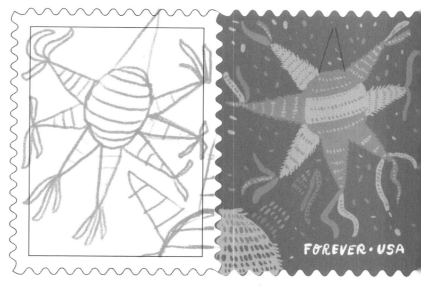

A significant part of many celebrations in Mexico and the United States, piñatas feature in all manner of festivities: holidays, birthdays, anniversaries, and weddings. They are also a traditional part of the *posadas*, a nine-day festival held in early December that commemorates Mary and Joseph's journey to Bethlehem before the birth of Jesus.

To create the stamps, artist and designer Víctor Meléndez drew on childhood memories. The four digital illustrations feature two traditional piñata designs — a donkey and a seven-point star. "I remember around Christmas my family would always break a star piñata," recalls Meléndez, "so I definitely wanted to include one in the art." Meléndez, who grew up in Mexico, says that the stamps' bright, saturated color palette was inspired by Mexican culture, including the vibrant colors of small-town houses, traditional hand-sewn dresses, handmade toys and flowers, and classic piñatas themselves.

Piñatas may have originated in China, where one new year's custom included beating an animal figurine with a stick until it broke open, releasing seeds from its hollow interior. In the 14th century, Italians used an undecorated clay vessel, the *pignatta* ("fragile pot"), filled with sweets rather than seeds, during Lenten celebrations. The practice migrated to Spain, and the pignatta — piñata in Spanish — was later brought to the Americas, where European missionaries found similar Indigenous traditions.

Whether a piñata is machine-made or crafted by hand, the customs surrounding it today are very similar to those from centuries ago. Filled with treats and presents, the piñata hangs by ropes while blindfolded players take turns striking it with a stick until the piñata breaks, scattering its contents on the ground to be gathered up by all the participants. Though the meaning of breaking the piñata has evolved, the result is still the same: bounty for all.

SNOW GLOBES

ART DIRECTOR & DESIGNER
DERRY NOYES

ARTIST
GREGORY MANCHESS

PLACE & DATE OF ISSUE
**BRECKENRIDGE, CO
SEPTEMBER 19, 2023**

Beloved by children and adults alike, snow globes can be miniature works of art, kitschy souvenirs, or anything in between. Holiday snow globes, vintage and modern, are favorites among collectors. The figures or panels inside might be anything related to Christmas: Santa Claus, reindeer, elves, popular holiday movie characters, a family gathered around a Christmas tree, or a tiny forest of firs waiting for a snowfall.

Inspired by a lifelong love of snow and the winter holiday season, artist Gregory Manchess reproduced the magic of Christmas sparkle held within four tiny, encapsulated landscapes. Painting in oil, he created the designs featuring seasonal icons.

Each spherical snow globe sits on a brown base. To get the reflection on the glass just right, Manchess studied actual snow globes. His last step was to add the snowflakes. "Snow is like fog," he explains. "It hides things and makes the world mysterious, giving it a unique and fresh perspective."

When a snow globe is shaken, the flitter — the technical term for the "snow" — creates a storm that briefly obscures the inside of the container. With one shake, the snowy interior becomes a miniature holiday celebration.

"The magic is in the light," reflects Manchess, "the way it plays on surfaces and reflects colors in unexpected ways. Capturing the light keeps the magic frozen in time."

> "Snow is like fog. It makes the world mysterious, giving it a unique and fresh perspective."
>
> — *Gregory Manchess, artist*

WINTER WOODLAND ANIMALS

Easily spotted across much of the North American landscape, deer, rabbits, owls, and foxes connect us to the natural beauty of the winter season.

These stamps feature whimsical, graphic illustrations of an antlered brown and white deer, a rust-colored fox, a snowy rabbit, and a bright-eyed owl. Depicted in geometric shapes of bold, solid color, each animal appears with details of its habitat in winter such as a full or crescent moon, snow-covered trees, holly branches with berries, and delicate snowflakes.

Illustrator Katie Kirk began by creating a series of small sketches exploring the subject as well as general layout and form before completing the art digitally.

"I played around with a bunch of different animals, including a bear, a goose, and an adorable white ermine, which I had a hard time letting go of," she explains. "Ultimately, I feel like the four animals we landed on will resonate the most with people. They have a quiet calm to them that I like. They speak to me of the magic of winter — of beauty in the cold."

ART DIRECTOR & DESIGNER
ANTONIO ALCALÁ

DESIGNER & ILLUSTRATOR
KATIE KIRK

PLACE & DATE OF ISSUE
WOODLAND, MI
OCTOBER 10, 2023

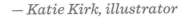

"Ultimately, I feel like the four animals we landed on will resonate the most with people. They have a quiet calm to them that I like. They speak to me of the magic of winter — of beauty in the cold."

— *Katie Kirk, illustrator*

SAILBOATS

ART DIRECTOR
ANTONIO ALCALÁ

DESIGNER, ILLUSTRATOR, & TYPOGRAPHER
LIBBY VANDERPLOEG

PLACE & DATE OF ISSUE
LAHAINA, HI
JANUARY 22, 2023

A sailing adventure offers a fun way to spend time with family and friends. Whether by ocean, lake, or river, sailing offers an opportunity to travel with your only company the creak of the lines, the flutter of the sails, and the lapping of waves against the hull.

Illustrator, Libby VanderPloeg grew up in a little harbor town on Lake Michigan. "There were always catamarans racing along the coast, and I loved seeing all the colorful sails set against the horizon," she remembers. "The water is such a peaceful place to spend time."

With these fond memories in mind, VanderPloeg created two colorful, graphic images that capture the essence of sailing, one of America's favorite pastimes.

RED FOX

ART DIRECTOR & DESIGNER
ETHEL KESSLER

EXISTING ART BY
DUGALD STERMER

PLACE & DATE OF ISSUE
FOX, AR
JANUARY 5, 2023

With a range that covers almost all of the United States except Hawai'i and parts of the Southwest, the intelligent and highly adaptable red fox *(Vulpes vulpes)* is well known to Americans coast to coast. It is found not only in woodlands and open country but also in suburbs and cities.

The stamp features a pencil-and-watercolor illustration by wildlife artist Dugald Stermer, admired by art director Ethel Kessler for his ability to infuse each subject with dignity. "I love that part of his style was to engage the animal with direct eye contact," says Kessler, "and I think that's what makes this image so special."

SCHOOL BUS

ART DIRECTOR
GREG BREEDING

DESIGNER / ARTIST
MIKE RYAN / STEVE WOLF

PLACE & DATE OF ISSUE
HIGH POINT, NC
JANUARY 5, 2023

Yellow school buses safely transport millions of children to and from school every day. The modern, enclosed, steel school bus first came into use in 1930. Its standard color, "School Bus Chrome," dates to 1939. The stamp features a stylized illustration of a 21st-century school bus by artist Steve Wolf.

"The size restriction forced me to distill the essence of a school bus into simple shapes and lines rather than showing every detail," Wolf explains. Silhouetted behind the modern bus is a schoolhouse evocative of an earlier era.

$10 FLORAL GEOMETRY

ART DIRECTOR
ANTONIO ALCALÁ

DESIGNER, ARTIST, & TYPOGRAPHER
SPAETH HILL

PLACE & DATE OF ISSUE
SAN DIEGO, CA
FEBRUARY 24, 2023

The art for this unique and beautiful stamp features a series of overlapping geometric shapes, including circles, ovals, triangles, and stars, that mimic the natural symmetry of floral patterns in their simplest forms. The red watercolor background, which was painted by hand and then scanned, imbues the stamp with a hint of sophistication.

The *$10 Floral Geometry* stamp complements the similarly designed $2 and $5 stamps issued in 2022. As the stamp denominations rise from $2 to $10, the designs become more complex. All of the stamps were printed with a foil treatment that adds an elegant glimmer to the design.

FLORIDA EVERGLADES

ART DIRECTOR & DESIGNER
GREG BREEDING

ARTIST
DAN COSGROVE

PLACE & DATE OF ISSUE
HOMESTEAD, FL
JANUARY 22, 2023

Spanning some two million acres in southern Florida, the Everglades is one of the largest wetlands in the world and the most significant breeding ground for tropical wading birds in North America.

The artwork shows a stand of mature bald cypress trees sheltering a great egret in flight. Nearby, a great blue heron awaits its prey as a half-submerged American alligator — a keystone species in the Everglades — moves through the shallow water.

"The evening light with the dark trees helps frame the image and draws the eye to the sunset sky in the distance," explains artist Dan Cosgrove. There, roseate spoonbills and other waterbirds fly overhead as the marsh meanders ever so slowly toward the horizon.

GREAT SMOKY MOUNTAINS

ART DIRECTOR & DESIGNER
GREG BREEDING

ARTIST
DAN COSGROVE

PLACE & DATE OF ISSUE
GATLINBURG, TN
JANUARY 22, 2023

Stretched along the border of Tennessee and North Carolina, the Smokies are home to extensive national forests and the largest protected bear habitat in the eastern United States. Humans have also inhabited this region for thousands of years, and their culture is preserved in heritage centers and interpreted in Great Smoky Mountains National Park.

The stamp art captures an iconic mountain scene located near Newfound Gap between Gatlinburg, Tennessee, and Cherokee, North Carolina. Artist Dan Cosgrove began with a pencil sketch, which he then scanned and finished digitally. To create a sense of movement and incorporate wildlife into the scene, Cosgrove added a red-tailed hawk flying high above the mountains.

ABOUT THE ART DIRECTORS

Antonio Alcalá
Drawing on his experience as a book designer and graphic designer, Antonio Alcalá served on the Postmaster General's Citizens' Stamp Advisory Committee in 2010 and 2011 before becoming an art director for the U.S. Postal Service stamp program.

Greg Breeding
Greg Breeding studied design and typography at Virginia Commonwealth University. His first stamp as an art director for the U.S. Postal Service was the 2012 issuance featuring the USS *Constitution*, the most famous ship of the War of 1812.

William Gicker
As Director of Stamp Services for the U.S. Postal Service, William Gicker oversees stamp development, stamp products and exhibitions, stamp manufacturing, stamp fulfillment, and the Postmaster General's Citizens' Stamp Advisory Committee.

Ethel Kessler
Ethel Kessler is an award-winning designer and art director who has worked with numerous corporations, museums, public and private institutions, and professional service organizations. She has been an art director for the U.S. Postal Service's stamp program for more than 25 years.

Derry Noyes
Derry Noyes has designed and provided art direction for dozens of United States postage stamps and stamp products for more than 35 years. Before becoming an art director for the Postal Service, she served as a member of the Citizens' Stamp Advisory Committee from 1981 to 1983.

ABOUT THE ARTISTS & ILLUSTRATORS

Carol Beehler
Patriotic Block
Graphic artist Carol Beehler specializes in the design of books, catalogues, magazines, brochures, and exhibition-related materials. She worked for many years as a book designer at the Smithsonian Institution Press and later as art director for publications at the Freer and Sackler Galleries.

Thomas Blackshear II
Chief Standing Bear
Known for his dramatic lighting and sensitivity to mood, Thomas Blackshear II has produced illustrations for stamps, posters, collectors' plates, magazines, greeting cards, calendars, books, and advertising. He has received many awards for his art including a gold medal from the Society of Illustrators.

Chris Buzelli
Love
Chris Buzelli exhibits his original oil paintings in galleries worldwide. He has received the Cube Award from The Art Directors Club and multiple medals from the Society of Illustrators. He teaches and gives lectures, workshops, and demonstrations at universities and conferences throughout the world.

Camille Chew
Lunar New Year • Year of the Rabbit
Since finishing college, Camille Chew has been working as a printmaker, exhibiting artist, and freelance illustrator. A magical flair gives her art a quirky sensibility while clean lines provide a contemporary take on her subjects.

Dan Cosgrove
Florida Everglades and *Great Smoky Mountains*
In 1980, Dan Cosgrove began a freelance career in digital and traditional illustration. He has illustrated more than 30 Priority Mail® and Priority Mail Express® stamps for the U.S. Postal Service.

Michael J. Deas
Ruth Bader Ginsburg
Michael J. Deas is an award-winning illustrator and master realist artist. For more than 20 years he has created stamp images for the U.S. Postal Service. His 1995 portrait of Marilyn Monroe became one of the top-selling commemorative stamps ever.

Alan Dingman
OSIRIS-REx
Alan Dingman is an illustrator, designer, and painter trained at Parsons School of Design and Rhode Island School of Design. His art has graced the covers of novels by *New York Times* best-selling authors Fredrik Backman, John Irving, David McCullough, and Ruth Ware, among others.

Down the Street Designs
Railroad Stations
Down the Street Designs is a creative studio based in Los Angeles, California, that specializes in illustration and animation.

Di'Orr Greenwood
Art of the Skateboard
Di'Orr Greenwood was born in northeastern Arizona, within the Navajo Nation. She takes pride in her tribal membership and her Diné upbringing. A skilled woodworker, she passes her techniques and philosophies along to community members through her products and instruction.

Katie Kirk
Winter Woodland Animals
Katie Kirk was drawn to animals and wildlife from an early age. Specializing in bold colors and playful geometry, she is often inspired by folk art and mid-century design, and cooking and nature are repeated themes in her work.

Noah MacMillan (1988–2022)
Women's Soccer
Noah MacMillan liked to make drawings that told stories and elicited feelings through simple design and obsessive attention to color. His work has been recognized by *Communication Arts*, American Illustration, *Print Magazine*, and the Society of Illustrators of Los Angeles.

Gregory Manchess
Snow Globes
Painter Gregory Manchess has worked as a freelance illustrator for more than 40 years on advertising campaigns, magazines, and book covers. He lectures frequently at universities and colleges nationwide, gives painting workshops, and teaches illustration.

MasPaz (Federico Frum)
Art of the Skateboard
Federico Frum, who works under the name MasPaz, is an artist, educator, and community activist whose murals and other artworks can be seen around the world. The distinctive thick lines he employs evoke Indigenous styles of the Americas, reflecting his deep affinity with these cultures.

Víctor Meléndez
Piñatas!
Originally from Mexico City, Víctor Meléndez is a designer and artist based in Seattle, Washington. A combination of bold lines, vivid colors, organic forms, and mysterious, spellbinding characters, Meléndez's work reflects his multicultural upbringing.

Robert Peterson
Ernest J. Gaines
Specializing in figure painting with an emphasis on portraiture, Robert Peterson has earned praise for his empowering depictions of people of color. His paintings have been exhibited at major art fairs in Miami, New York, Chicago, and Los Angeles.

Mike Ryan
Ernest J. Gaines and *School Bus*
Mike Ryan serves as the Principal Designer and Editorial Studio Director for the design agency Journey Group. The *Edgar Allan Poe* commemorative booklet, which he designed for the U.S. Postal Service, was featured in the *PRINT* Regional Design Annual and the *HOW* International Design Annual.

Spaeth Hill
$10 Floral Geometry
Founded in 2017 by Jill Spaeth and Nathan Hill, Spaeth Hill is a contemporary design practice that specializes in experiential graphic design, wayfinding, branding, and publication design.

Ellen Surrey
Thinking of You
As an illustrator, Ellen Surrey combines her love of bright colors, mid-century design, and children's books from the 1950s and 1960s to create nostalgic yet contemporary designs. She recently illustrated several children's books, including biographies of Dolly Parton and Babe Ruth.

William James Taylor Junior
Art of the Skateboard
Pop culture–inspired line drawings, vivid color palettes, and kaleidoscopic psychedelia typify the artwork of William James Taylor Junior. The mesmerizing creations of this self-taught Norfolk, Virginia, artist can be seen emblazoned on skateboards, casual clothing, and prints.

Libby VanderPloeg
Sailboats
Libby VanderPloeg describes her style as whimsical, colorful, bold, and modern. She especially enjoys playing with pattern, and making colorful, detailed maps. Her work has also appeared in numerous national publications.

Steve Wolf
School Bus
A designer and illustrator, Steve Wolf creates works that convey simplicity and sophistication. His unique style blends vintage-inspired design, modern elements, and just the right amount of whimsy.

Crystal Worl
Art of the Skateboard
Crystal Worl is a Tlingit/Athabascan designer. With her brother, Rico, she is the co-founder of Trickster Company, which promotes innovative Indigenous design. Her work explores the relationships and bonds between her people, the land, and animals.

ACKNOWLEDGMENTS

Louis DeJoy
Postmaster General and Chief Executive Officer

Steven W. Monteith
Chief Customer and Marketing Officer and
Executive Vice President

Sheila B. Holman
Vice President, Marketing

William Gicker
Director, Stamp Services

Shawn Quinn
Manager, Stamp Development

Lisa Albright
Program Manager

Journey Group
Creative Development and Design

Clare LaVergne, PhotoAssist, Inc.
Writer and Editor

Michael Owens, PhotoAssist, Inc.
Image Research, Rights and Permissions

Mary Stephanos, PhotoAssist, Inc.
Writer and Editor

John Roberts Printing
Minneapolis, Minnesota
Production

The Postal Service™ would like to thank the
members of the Citizens' Stamp Advisory
Committee for their contributions to the
2023 stamp program. For more information
about the members of CSAC, please visit:
about.usps.com/who/csac

CREDITS

Cover
Photographs by Don Komarechka

Copyright and Table of Contents
Clockwise from top left, photographs by
Steve Gschmeissner; Igor Siwanowicz (2);
and Tagide deCarvalho

Page 4 / Photograph by Charles B. Krebs

Page 5 / Photograph by Steve Gschmeissner

Commemorative Stamps / Section Divider
Photograph by Igor Siwanowicz

Lunar New Year • Year of the Rabbit
Page 9 / Art by Camille Chew,
© 2023 U.S. Postal Service

Ernest J. Gaines
Page 10 / Photograph by Raoul Benavides; sketch
by Robert Peterson, © 2023 U.S. Postal Service

Women's Soccer
Page 13 / Art by Noah MacMillan,
© 2023 U.S. Postal Service

Toni Morrison
Page 14 / Photograph by Dwight Carter

Railroad Stations
Page 17 / Photograph by Clifton H. Williams II;
art by Down the Street Designs,
© 2023 U.S. Postal Service

Page 18 / Photograph by Larry Helms;
sketches by Down the Street Designs,
© 2023 U.S. Postal Service

Page 19 / Preliminary stamp designs by Down
the Street Designs, © 2023 U.S. Postal Service;
photograph by Wes Taylor

Art of the Skateboard
Page 20 / Photograph by Crystal Worl

Page 22 / Photograph by Donavan Johnson

Page 23 / Photographs by Albert "Pootie" Ting;
Linnea Bullion; and Tofurious Maximus Crane

Roy Lichtenstein
Page 25 / Photograph ©Bob Adelman;
Art © 2022 Estate of Roy Lichtenstein.
All rights reserved.

Tomie dePaola
Page 28 / Whitebird, Inc.

Chief Standing Bear
Page 31 / Nebraska State Historical Society
Photograph Collections

Endangered Species
Pages 32 and 34 / Photographs by Joel Sartore

Waterfalls
Page 37 / Photograph by QT Luong

Page 38 / Clockwise from top, photographs
by QT Luong; Joe Miller; Kenneth Keifer;
and Sandra Woods

John Lewis
Page 40 / Photographs by Audra Melton (top)
and Steve Schapiro

Life Magnified
Page 43 / Photograph by Igor Siwanowicz

Page 44 / Clockwise from top left, photographs
by Igor Siwanowicz; Tagide deCarvalho;
Daniel Castranova; and David Liittschwager

Thinking of You
Page 46 / Art by Ellen Surrey,
© 2023 U.S. Postal Service

OSIRIS-REx
Page 49 / Art by Alan Dingman,
© 2023 U.S. Postal Service

Ruth Bader Ginsburg
Page 50 / Sketch by Michael J. Deas,
© 2023 U.S. Postal Service;
photograph by Stephanie Maze

Mail-Use Stamps / Section Divider
Photograph by Jason Kirk

Love
Page 54 / Sketches by Chris Buzelli,
© 2023 U.S. Postal Service

Piñatas!
Page 57 / Sketches by Víctor Meléndez,
© 2023 U.S. Postal Service

Snow Globes
Page 58 / Sketches by Gregory Manchess,
© 2023 U.S. Postal Service

Winter Woodland Animals
Page 59 / Sketches by Katie Kirk,
© 2023 U.S. Postal Service

Great Smoky Mountains
Page 61 / Sketches by Dan Cosgrove,
© 2023 U.S. Postal Service